COMPASSIONATE
ENQUIRY

A manager's guide to addressing conduct and performance issues in the workplace.

Andrew E. Colsky

JD, LLM, LPC

Dedication

To my family and friends, work colleagues (too many to mention) and teachers; thank you for sharing your wisdom with me and encouraging me to strive for continuous improvement. It is that wisdom that came together piece by piece over the years that helped me create the contents of this book. I consider this work as a collective made up from my experiences and exchanges with my entire personal community.

Contents

CHAPTER 1:

Perspective

In life, there is one thing we carry with us everywhere we go, every minute of the day and it is unique only to us. It shapes our world and our reactions to that world. That thing is our perspective. It is based upon a lifetime collection of our own unique experiences and it shapes how we see and respond to the world and the people around us.

Employees, coworkers, supervisors, managers and anyone else in the workplace come to work each day carrying their perspectives. Every conversation they have, every action they take and every reaction they have is first filtered through the lens of their perspective. Perspective allows for uniqueness and differences. The ability to see things differently is what allows us to be creative and invent new products and processes. Perspective can also be the foundation of misunderstandings or well understood disagreements.

Healthy relationships are built upon the ability to understand another's perspective and appreciate their responses given that understanding. Successful managers learn this early on. The best way to encourage an employee to buy-in to a task is to present it in a way they can appreciate it from their own perspective. After all, it's not very hard to convince someone to do something they want to do yet it can seem nearly impossible to try to get them to do something they do not want to do. This is the essence of persuasion.

Sometimes there are managers who don't understand the power of perspective. They are under the impression that their title simply bestows upon them a great power and that is all they need to force their employees to comply with their every demand. These managers ultimately fail but they can leave a long line of destruction in their path.

Unfortunately, even the well-intentioned manager who tries to support their employees can run into troubles when they fail to understand each employee's perspective. These managers cannot be faulted for their actions, they simply have never received training on how they can gain the benefit of their employees unique perspective.

When a manager finds him or herself in need of addressing a conduct or performance issue, their first inclination is to refer to the company human resource policies and proceed as directed. While many companies are continuing to improve their processes, it is not uncommon for an employer to simply address these issues through a series of steps referred to as progressive discipline. Progressive discipline is merely a series of administrative steps, each with progressively harsher punishments bestowed upon an employee to force them into operating under the rules established by their employer.

In my over 30 years of experience, I have found that progressive discipline policies do not account for an employee's perspective, nor do they have any effective provisions to address an employee who may not currently be in a mentally healthy state. I use the term "mentally healthy" instead of the term "mental health" to make a point. We all have days when we simply are not at our best and could not be considered "mentally healthy" even though we do not have a diagnosable mental health condition.

An employee does not have to have a diagnosable mental health condition to come to work mentally unhealthy. Consider the mother who is working in a management role and briefing her employees when she receives a telephone call from the school that her child has had an accident. She is told that her child will be OK as he merely has a bad cut on his leg but her perspective has now changed for the day. It would be hard to argue that this mother would be mentally healthy after receiving such a phone call. If an employee is unaware of this mothers situation and approaches her with a complaint about the copier toner being empty yet again, it would not be difficult to see how this mother might snap back with an impatient response even though she normally is very calm and collected. Had that employee understood this mothers current perspective, they may have chosen to forgo the comment or waited for a different time.

The passages below introduce us to Charlene and Charles and give us an understanding of each of their perspectives on the same set of circumstances. The situation is based on reality and may even be recognizable to the reader in one form or another.

Charlene

Charlene was very proud today. After 5 long years of hard work, she had finally been promoted to supervisor at one of the nation's largest fulfillment companies. She was excited to have completed supervisor training and was ready to build a high performing team. The future was looking bright.

Charlene's Manager, Sam, introduced her to her new team of five fulfillment specialists, most of whom she had known for the last few years. She knew they were all good people and she also knew that some of them had also competed for her job. She didn't expect this to be a problem as many people had been promoted to supervisor by rising up in the ranks as she had done. The others would have their chance.

The first few weeks on the job, Charlene got comfortable with her role and all of her subordinates really seemed to take a liking to her style. Charlene was fair but firm. Not too firm as to turn her employees against her but firm enough to keep performance and spirits up.

Charlene was proud when one of her subordinates, Charles, announced to his coworkers that his wife was pregnant. They were expecting twins! The whole team got together and threw him a baby shower the next week and Charlene brought one of her often raved about and well-loved peach cobblers. Things could not be going better.

Over the next few months, Charlene did have to speak with one of her employees about their performance and had to resolve a pay error for another but these were all things she was trained to do. As the weeks passed, three of Charlene's subordinates approached her with complaints that Charles was not pulling his weight. They told her that he just didn't seem to be able to keep up the enthusiasm that she had built ever since she became supervisor.

Charlene approached Charles in passing and half-jokingly said to him "come on man, we've got to keep up the spirit." At another point about a week later, she saw him looking a bit distracted and said "focus man, I know you can do it."

She thought that all Charles needed was a little encouragement. Afterall, a fulfillment specialist's job can get tedious at times.

Another few weeks went by and Charles 'co-workers approached Charlene with some more frustration about his performance. Apparently Charles just didn't seem to care much about his job anymore. Charlene's numbers were slipping because Charles wasn't keeping pace. Poor numbers affected the whole team and now she had the beginnings of a morale problem.

Charlene referred to her supervisor training manual and realized that she had to take action to get Charles back in the game. She re-read the company's progressive discipline policy and saw that the first step was to speak with the employee about the issue. Well, Charlene figured that she had already spoken to Charles twice. She told him to "keep up the spirit" and "I know you can do it" but neither seemed to change things.

The second step in the progressive discipline process was to issue a Letter of Warning. Charlene had never drafted a Letter of Warning before so she met with her Manager and asked if he could help her draft the letter this first time. Sam coached Charlene through the process and Charlene was careful to be fair and honest in the letter. She met with Charles the next day and sat him down in a private room, just like the manual suggested and she issued him the Letter of Warning. She assumed that this was all that Charles would need to convince him to "get back in the game" is how she put it when speaking with him.

To Charlene's dismay, Charles did not "get back in the game." In fact, things seemed to be getting worse, not better. Now, even Charlene noticed how Charles seemed to be "checked-out" from his job. He worked as if he was fighting inertia. His numbers were way down and the team continued to suffer. Charlene had tried to correct the problem but now she was feeling disrespected. Charles was making her look bad. She worked hard to become a supervisor and she had every intention of proving herself and becoming a manager in two years.

Charlene had heard about other supervisors who experienced similar employee issues. She never thought that she would actually have to deal with this herself one day. Charlene didn't know what else to do so she turned back to her supervisor training and it took her back to the next step of the progressive discipline. Charlene trusted the process; afterall, it was written by a team of human resource experts. While she didn't want to have to move to the next step which was to send Charles home for one day without pay, she had to correct this problem.

Charlene reluctantly met with Human Resources and drafted the paperwork to issue Charles a one day suspension without pay. Paperwork in hand, she met with

Charles again in private and told him how disappointed she was in his performance and that it had to improve because he was bringing the whole team down. She told him she was sending him home for one day without pay and expected him to come back to work the day after next and "get his head back in the game." If he was unable to comply, she informed him that the next steps in the progressive discipline process could eventually lead to his removal.

Charles left that day and seemed changed when he returned to work. Charlene didn't know what happened until a week later when her Manager told her that Charles had filed a harassment complaint against the company with the Equal Employment Opportunity Commission. Charlene was scared; was she responsible for getting her company in trouble with the law? Afterall, she followed the rules and did exactly what her company trained her to do. What went wrong? Was she going to be in trouble? Surely her dreams of becoming manager in two years were ruined. What a mess!

Charles

Charles had just graduated from high school and things were looking up. He married his high school sweetheart, Barbara and they found a great little apartment in a beautiful neighborhood with a park right outside their front door. Charles had been looking for work and found a job at the local fulfillment center which was one of the largest employers in the area. The company was known for good pay and employees seemed to enjoy working there.

Barbara wasn't working at the time. Their plan was to start a family while Barbara stayed at home to raise the kids. Once the kids were of school age, she would begin to work to help supplement the family income.

Charles began work and really seemed to enjoy his job and his coworkers. He was on a large team with what he felt were too many coworkers for him to ever be recognized. When the manager, Sam, came to him one day and said that he was going to reassign Charles to a new, smaller team of five fulfillment specialists under a new supervisor, Charles thought this would be a great way for him to finally stand out above the crowd.

Charles was very happy when he came to work one day and Sam introduced a new supervisor, Charlene, who was going to be leading a small team of five fulfillment specialists, of which Charles was a part. Charles felt as if his life plan was all coming together. He graduated from high school, got married to a wonderful woman, Barbara, moved into a new, beautiful apartment across from a park, got a great job with a good company, and now was in a position at work where he could be noticed and potentially move up more quickly.

Charles really seemed to enjoy working with Charlene because she was nice to him and had a reputation as "firm but fair." When Barbara announced to Charles that she was pregnant with twins, he couldn't wait to share the news with Charlene and his coworkers. He was even more elated when his coworkers threw him a baby shower and his supervisor took the time to make one of her prized peach cobblers for him.

Things were going great at home and things were going great at work. Charles couldn't be happier. Then came the news. Barbara had gone in for a regular checkup and the doctor discovered there might be serious problems with one of the twins. Charles was devastated.

Things were moving fast at home while Charles and Barbara worked with the doctors to try and sort out any potential problems. This meant a lot of tests, a lot of expense and a lot of stress. Charles did not want to share any of this with his workplace because he wasn't even sure what was happening himself. He tried to keep his mind on work but all he could think about was what was happening with his twins.

Charles didn't realize that the stress he was under was affecting his job performance. He knew that he didn't have the same pep in his step that he usually brought to work but he thought that he was still performing up to expectations. He knows that Charlene had made some comments about "keeping up the spirit" and telling him to "focus" but he really didn't think much of them because he knew that she was always trying to encourage everyone on the team to keep performance up.

At this point, Charles was starting to feel defeated. His babies 'health was in the hands of the doctors, medical bills were starting to pile up and he felt like he had nowhere to turn. At least he had a stable job with medical insurance that was going to help him through this difficult time. If he could just make it through the birth of his babies, he felt that things would start to turn around.

Charles came into work the next day and was completely caught off guard when his supervisor, Charlene asked to speak with him privately. She gave him a letter of warning and told him that he needed to improve his performance. Charles was hurt and offended and figured it was best to simply sign the letter and get out of there as soon as he could that day.

Charles was doing everything in his power to keep his life together. He had to be the mental support for his wife, Barbara who was having a hard time processing all that was happening to her unborn children. She was depressed and he often found her sitting, crying. He also had to keep up appearances at work because he didn't want anybody to know what was going on at home. The truth is, even if he wanted to share, he wasn't sure that he knew enough about the situation to share any meaningful information.

It seemed as if the walls were closing in on Charles as he waited for the results of the next round of medical tests. These tests should be able to inform him whether he could expect his children to be carried to term or whether his wife would need an emergency C-section. Charles was completely blindsided when he came into work the next day and Charlene again asked to speak with him privately. This time, she gave Charles a one day unpaid suspension and informed him that if he didn't "get it together", he could even be terminated.

Charles was hurt, shocked, angry and frustrated all at the same time. He had worked so hard at his job and in his greatest time of need, he was being treated like dirt. He couldn't afford to lose one day's worth of pay and he certainly couldn't afford to lose his job. He wasn't sure what to do. He was working as hard as he could, he always got to work on time and always stayed to the end of his shift. What more did they want?

Charles shared his situation with his best friend Chris who convinced Charles that he needed to stand up for himself and fight back or he could find himself without a job. Charles was very scared because he could not afford to lose his job or his health insurance. Out of desperation Charles contacted an attorney who convinced him to file a claim with the Equal Employment Opportunity Commission (EEOC) for harassment. He had never thought about starting any trouble with his employer but the fear of losing his job and his insurance was too great a risk. He had no choice.

Charles returned to work and realized one day that Charlene had been informed about his claim with the EEOC, because she seemed very on-edge and wasn't sure how to act around him. He felt terrible but there was no way he was going to allow her to jeopardize his salary and health insurance. He had to file the claim because Charlene had given him no choice.

CHAPTER 2:
Compassionate Enquiry

The case example between Charles and Charlene is very real. I came to realize this early on when I was learning how to handle employment claims as a young attorney. I had many employees approach me with similar stories and seek advice on what they could do to protect their jobs. I also spoke with many employers who were frustrated and concerned about how they could encourage their employees to better perform.

The common thread I found in almost all cases was that the current legal advice at the time was to inform the employer and employee to let the lawyers handle it and refrain from speaking with each other. The lawyers would soldier on using what they learned in law school to zealously advocate for their client's interests. The actual parties, in this case, Charles and Charlene, were simply instructed not to speak with each other and were basically left out of the process.

Charles and Charlene would have to continue to work together on a daily basis while at the same time hearing from their attorneys about how Charles needed to fight for his rights and Charlene would need to protect her employer. The workplace relationship became hostile and all of the employees on the team would suffer. In the end, nobody ever really won in these cases. Expensive legal fees eventually would force one or the other side to give in and settle the claim.

The main lesson that I learned was that almost all of the cases that I handled could have been prevented if management and the employee had simply spoken with each other about the situation. These conversations began to occur as the concept of alternative dispute resolution and specifically mediation became more accepted as useful in resolving employment claims. Mediation proved to be the standard bearer in this arena and I personally have successfully mediated employment claims for over 30 years.

As I began to consult with employers about how to minimize employment claims, I encouraged them to train their supervisors and managers in appropriate communication skills. Proper training would equip them to address employee problems at their inception. There was no reason to wait for tensions to boil over and a legal claim to be filed.

The biggest challenge I faced was how to train the managers and supervisors to hold an effective conversation. Simply informing them to communicate with their subordinates was not enough. Many of them simply did not have the skills on how to speak with their subordinates in a way that would not inflame tensions.

As I studied the problem, the number one error that I found in these conversations was that the manager or supervisor would approach the employee to talk yet fail to ask for the employee's perspective. Without the benefit of knowledge of the employee's perspective, management would have to rely on their own perspective which, by default requires them to make an assumption about the employee's perspective. Once the manager or supervisor learned to ask the employee for an explanation for their actions, the situation often became easier to resolve.

It is important for everyone, management and employee, to realize that we never know what is going on in someone's life. We see the part that they let us see but we are in the dark as to the big picture. Are there employees who are just not good performers? Sure there are. However, in most of the situations that I have encountered, there is an element of some sort of distress, often with a direct or ancillary connection to an employees mental wellness.

When people are stressed, they seek ways to cope. Some people internalize their problems and try to conduct business as usual. Others may shut down or turn to alcohol or drugs to numb their feelings. Often when an employer recognizes an issue with an employee's conduct or performance, if they effectively seek the employee's perspective, both the cause of the problem and the solution become clear.

Compassionate Enquiry is a framework for an effective conversation that any manager or supervisor can use to address an employee with conduct or performance issues. I developed this process based on my over 30 years of experience working with employment disputes at some of the largest workplaces in the world. I have applied my legal and mental health expertise to carefully craft each step of the process and then perfect it over several years of use. I am extremely pleased with the results that I see and I am consistently contacted by managers who express how their use of this process has made their job much easier and more rewarding.

The Compassionate Enquiry Process

The Compassionate Enquiry process is based on a framework consisting of five steps. The steps can be easily remembered by the acronym I-CARE. The steps are:

- I - Initiate

- C - Clarify

- A - Acknowledge

- R - Resolve

- E - Eye-to-Eye

In the next chapters I will walk the reader through each and every step of the framework. The process is quite simple yet it's development was quite complex. Any manager or supervisor who follows the process as written, will find it easy and rewarding to have a meaningful conversation with any employee exhibiting a conduct or performance issue.

I realize there will be skeptics. I hear from them every time I teach the model. I also know that those skeptics become believers once they see the process in action. I would expect that some of you reading this book will also approach the subject with a healthy dose of skepticism. You may be thinking to yourself, "yes, but I have an employee with which this would never work." I have heard all of the concerns and almost all of the skeptics end up embracing the power of Compassionate Enquiry.

Compassionate Enquiry

1. *I - Initiate*

   a. *"I would like to speak with you about (topic)."*
   b. *Follow with specific facts supporting your concerns.*

2. *C - Clarify*

   a. *"When you (do the thing we are discussing) it causes (the negative outcome I wish to avoid)"*
   b. *"Can you help me understand what is causing you to (do the things we are discussing)?*

3. *A - Acknowledge*

   a. *"I hear that you (paraphrase their perspective)."*
   b. *Be prepared to use the "A - Loop" if they deflect.*

4. *R - Resolve*

   a. *"How can we work together to resolve this issue?"*
   b. *Focus on interests, not positions to identify meaningful solutions.*

5. *E - Eye-to-eye*

   a. *"Please describe our understanding to me in your own words."*

CHAPTER 3:

Initiating the Conversation

"I" stands for "Initiate"

Which is the first step in the Compassionate Enquiry process. The initiation phase consists of two parts. First, the speaker makes a clear statement defining the topic of the discussion. The topic is then clarified by a more complete recitation of supporting facts.

1. "I would like to speak with you about (topic)."
2. (Recite supporting facts.)

The first two steps sound elementary but can actually take some effort to master. When you try to define the topic of the discussion, it can be quite difficult to remove your own biases and judgment. The topic of the discussion should be a simple, non-judgemental statement. Often, for the untrained, the topic ends up being phrased as an accusation.

Stating the Topic

The topic should neither state an accusation nor an assumption. It should merely lay the groundwork for the discussion by defining the subject matter to be discussed. Let's take a look at an example.

Larry works at a retail establishment in a busy shopping district. He is scheduled to work Monday through Friday from opening at 10:00 am until closing at 6:00 pm. For the entire first year of his employment, Larry has always arrived either on time or early. Over the last three weeks Larry has arrived on time with the following exceptions. Two weeks ago, Larry arrived late at 10:05 am on Tuesday. Last week he arrived at 10:15 am on Tuesday and again at 10:09 am on Thursday. Finally, this week, Larry arrived late again on Tuesday at 10:07 am and on Thursday at 10:20 am.

Larry's supervisor, Shannon decides that it is time to make a Compassionate Enquiry into Larry's actions. Shannon recently graduated from a Compassionate Enquiry course and she knows that she is supposed to "initiate" the conversation with Larry. She makes the following attempts.

Shannon: "Larry, you need to start getting up earlier and get here on time."

Larry: "What are you talking about? I get up at 7:30 am everyday, whether I like it or not!"

Well, that didn't go so well. A compassionate enquiry, when done correctly, will not spark an argument from step one. In fact, a compassionate enquiry will prevent an argument. In this case, Shannon was accusatory and assumed that the reason Larry was arriving late was that he was waking up late.

Shannon studied her notes about Compassionate Enquiry and started again.

Shannon: "Larry, you keep coming in late."

Larry: "I do not! I was only late once or twice."

Oops, Shannon did it again. She accused Larry of something and used vague language. What does "keep coming in late" actually mean? To Shannon, it appears to mean coming in late at least five times. But how does Larry define "keep coming in late?" The answer is that it doesn't matter. Shannon set herself up for a confrontation because she accused Larry of something and he defended himself.

Accusatory language is almost always met with a defensive response.

Shannon went back to the drawing board and reviewed the Compassionate Enquiry method a little bit closer this time. She was having a hard time accepting that stating the topic seemed to be quite difficult for something that should be so easy. Shannon figured that she needed to look at her attempts and break them down. She asked herself "What is the common theme behind all of my language?" Suddenly she realized that it was "attendance," she wanted to speak with Larry about his attendance. When Larry arrives to work late, he is displaying an attendance problem. She decided to give it one more try.

Shannon: "Larry, I would like to speak with you about your attendance."

Larry: "Sure, what's up?"

But wait, no argument? No pushback? No defensiveness? Well, there may be some defensiveness; after-all, Larry's boss has just told him that she would like to speak with him about his attendance. Shannon was not accusatory, nor did she state any assumptions so Larry was simply ready to listen to see where this conversation is going.

Is that all there is to stating the topic; one word, "attendance?" That seems so elementary yet it was so hard to arrive at. When it comes to stating the topic, the simpler the better.

We Need to Talk

It can be anxiety producing to think about approaching an employee to discuss a conduct or performance issue. If it is done wrong, it is easy for the conversation to quickly devolve into an argument. As we saw above, Shannon initially had a hard time even stating her first words without provoking an argumentative response. To avoid getting into an argument, some supervisors or managers opt to put off the inevitable conversation until they are ready. Unfortunately the desire to avoid an argument by putting it off until later can actually set the stage for a bigger argument once the conversation is had.

A common error made by managers when addressing an employee is to meet the employee at the beginning of their shift and state something along the lines of "we need to talk" or "see me later on your break" or any one of unlimited versions of this vague statement. Think about your perspective when hearing such a statement. Vague statements provoke anxiety in many people. Since anxiety comes from thoughts about something unknown in the future, people spend their time thinking about and trying to solve the mystery. Couple this anxiety with a general negativity bias many of us exhibit about the unknown and all we can do is start to imagine the worst.

If Shannon approached Larry and simply said "we need to talk later," it would not be illogical for Larry to start to think to himself things like "I'm in trouble" or "surely I'm going to be fired." This anxiety understandably builds over time as Larry ruminates over these thoughts and plans his defenses throughout the day. Finally, when Shannon calls Larry to her office, she could be setting a match to the powder keg her words created.

Supporting Facts

Let's revisit Shannon's topic statement. "Larry, I would like to speak with you about your attendance." The Initiation phase of every Compassionate Enquiry requires that the topic statement be followed immediately by the supporting facts. The hard part is that facts are often confused with vague statements, assumptions, accusations or hearsay. The easy part is that if you stick purely to the facts, you continue to set the proper stage for an effective conversation. The good news is that if you are initiating a Compassionate Enquiry, you are in total control of the Initiation phase.

Shannon is feeling confident because she received such a positive reaction to her topic statement. Larry was listening. Shannon decided it was time to start listing the facts.

Shannon: "You came in late several times in the last few weeks."

Larry: "No, I didn't."

Wait, what? Shannon was stunned, she stated the facts, didn't she? Larry was late several times in the last few weeks, wasn't he? Why is he sounding argumentative? Did Shannon misunderstand the Compassionate Enquiry process?

Shannon did make a factual statement but it was also filled with vague words open to interpretation. What does "several times" mean? How should she expect Larry to react when he is feeling on the spot when his boss is addressing him? Larry will probably define "several times" as meaning many more times than he was actually late. So, in his perspective, for "several times" to be true, it requires him to be late more times than he was. Thus, he is going to confidently answer exactly as he did. In his mind, he was not late "several times."

Shannon thought about it and realized that she made an error by using vague language. She would not make that mistake again. She decided to give it another try.

Shannon: "You need to start trying harder to get here on time."

Larry: "What are you talking about? I try very hard to get here on time."

Here we go again, what's wrong this time? Shannon made an unfounded accusation based on an assumption. She assumed that Larry was coming in late because he was not trying to get to work on time. She left herself fully vulnerable in this situation because she had no way of knowing if her assumptions were correct. Even if they were, she had no way to prove it. A proper statement of facts cannot be effectively challenged.

Shannon, not one to give up easily, tries one more time.

Shannon: "Scott told me you came in at 10:20 am this last Thursday."

Larry: "Why is it any of Scott's business?"

Well, that didn't go over well either. Shannon attributed her "facts" to a statement she heard from Scott. Such information is not a fact, it is what we call "hearsay." Hearsay is when someone accepts the statement of a third party and uses it to prove the facts of the matter asserted. In other words, Shannon accepted Scott's words as true and then used them as factual proof against Larry. Even if it is true that Larry arrived at work at 10:20 am last Thursday, Shannon's use of hearsay detracted from a solid statement of facts.

Shannon was confused. She tried three times and can't seem to make a proper statement of facts. Once again she returned to the drawing board and broke it down. She looked at the definition of a fact and found that facts are things that are known to be true. She also re-read the Compassionate Enquiry process and realized that the facts, as stated, need to be as specific as possible. Then suddenly it clicked! She knew what she was doing wrong. Now she was ready; she was sure of it.

She approached Larry and said:

Shannon: "Larry, I would like to speak with you about your attendance." She followed her topic statement with the following facts: "Your shift starts at 10:00 am. Two weeks ago on Tuesday, you arrived to work at 10:05 am. Last week you arrived at 10:15 am on Tuesday and at 10:09 am on Thursday. Finally, this week, you arrived on Tuesday at 10:07 am and on Thursday at 10:20 am.

Larry: "Yes, I understand."

Larry had no argument. Shannon approached him with a clear topic followed by specific facts and Larry stated that he understood. Is it really that simple?

It really is that simple. If Shannon had erred in her statement of specific facts, Larry would have probably corrected her. He may have said something like "I was here at 10:05 am on Tuesday, not 10:07." That is fine. Now,

Larry is telling Shannon that he does not disagree that he was late, he just wants the record to be clear on his actual time of arrival.

Having to provide a clear statement of specific facts helps the speaker to be sure to have their facts straight before approaching the listener and sets clear expectations for both parties as to what the conversation will address. By following the rules of the Initiation phase of a Compassionate Enquiry, the remainder of the conversation becomes focused and productive.

CHAPTER 4:

Gaining Clarity

In the initiation phase, you stated clearly both the topic of the conversation and the specific facts supporting the purpose of the conversation. The next step is to clarify why the conversation is important to you and to gain clarification from the other party about their actions. Thus, there are two distinct steps required when you clarify. First, you will explain why the issue is important enough for you to be addressing it. Next you will seek to gain a better understanding of the other person's actions by specifically asking for their explanation as to why they took their actions.

1. "When you (do the thing we are discussing) it causes (the negative outcome I wish to avoid)"

2. "Can you help me understand what is causing you to (do the things we are discussing)?

Why I Care

Shannon has initiated a conversation with Larry about his attendance. She provided specific factual information upon which she is relying including dates and times of his attendance issues. Now, she will explain to Larry why the issue of his attendance is of concern. Again, Shannon will refrain from using accusatory language or making assumptions about his intent. It is also important to remain inquisitive and open-minded.

Shannon: "It's a violation of company policy to arrive late. I don't want to have to write you up."

Larry: "I don't appreciate being threatened."

Now what? Shannon didn't state anything untrue. It is indeed a violation of company policy for an employee to arrive late. And it is also true that the company policy is to provide progressive discipline to employees who violate policy. So why did Larry respond so defensively?

Larry felt attacked. Shannon accused him of violating company policy and assumed he had a bad intent for doing so. She has no idea what is going on or why Larry has been late. Shannon decided to try again.

Shannon: "You need to figure out how to arrive at work on time."

Larry: "I know what I need to do, you don't have to beat me up about it."

Shannon used the phrase "you need" which Larry automatically received as accusatory. Even if Shannon restated her comment as "It is important to arrive at work on time" then she would have remained factual and Larry wouldn't have had anything to rebut. But even this is not the most effective way to explain why the issue is important enough for her to address it with him. A statement of fact is not an explanation of why the issue concerns her. If Shannon simply provides more information while refraining from making assumptions and avoiding accusatory language, perhaps it will go better.

Shannon: "When you arrive late, it leaves only one employee to work alone in the store. Not only does that severely limit our ability to provide excellent customer service but it can be dangerous because anyone can walk in off the street and cause harm. Also, our data shows that shoplifting increases when a single employee is busy with a customer and unable to supervise the store."

Larry: "Okay."

That went pretty well. Larry didn't complain or talk back because he didn't feel attacked. He has a clear understanding why the issue is important to Shannon and is signaling that he has heard her. Shannon now knows that she is ready to move to the next step in the Clarify stage.

Help me understand

Once Shannon has laid the groundwork and clarified her intent, she is now ready to ask Larry for his explanation of what is causing him to be late. One of the best ways to do this is to ask Larry to "help me understand what has caused you to arrive late?" Of course there are unlimited ways to ask this question and each person will have their own words. It is best to avoid using the word "why" because it can sound accusatory. Let's give it a try and see what happens.

Shannon: "Why can't you get here on time?"

Larry: "I do my best. What do you want from me?"

Here we go again. Shannon says something that Larry perceives as accusatory and he responds defensively. This conversation has little chance of being effective. The next words will probably be the beginning of an argument followed by a threat of discipline. Unfortunately, the problem has not been resolved and now Shannon and Larry's relationship has been damaged.

There has to be a better way. If Shannon uses respectful language, and simply asks Larry to help her understand what is making him late, he may feel comfortable enough to share the details of his situation with her.

Shannon: "Can you help me understand what has caused you to arrive to work late?"

Notice how Shannon was artful with her language. She didn't ask Larry "why" he was late, she asked what has caused him to be late. Substituting "what" for "why" can produce better responses because the person on the receiving end does not feel attacked or accused. Shannon is simply seeking facts.

Response Options

Employees at the clarifying stage of the process can respond in one of three ways:

1) Provide a reasonable explanation that accounts for their behavior and allows for a discussion on how to address it.

2) Provide an explanation that is true, yet demonstrates improper behavior and again allows for a discussion on how to address it, or

3) Deflect the question to avoid having to answer or provide an explanation.

Explanations

An employee can be struggling with mental health issues, problems at home, legal issues, physical health issues, etc. The point is that a manager has no way of knowing what is going on in an employee's life. The only way to know is to approach the situation compassionately and with an open mind. The manager should be curious and truly interested in learning about the situation. If the employee provides a vague response, it probably means that they are not sure if they can trust their manager yet. By demonstrating empathy and understanding, the manager may be able to create an environment where the employee feels safe enough to elaborate on their situation.

Sympathy, Empathy and Compassion

We often hear and use the words sympathy, empathy and compassion. If asked to define and differentiate between them, many people struggle.

Sympathy is having feelings for another. "I feel bad that my neighbor had a flood in their basement and lost some family heirlooms."

Empathy is the ability to understand and share the feelings of another. It can be described as if you "caught" the feelings from the other person. A person responds with empathy when they feel what the other person feels. "I understand how my neighbor feels about losing some family heirlooms in their flooded basement. I felt the same way when my hard drive crashed and I lost some of my cherished family photos."

Compassion is an expression of empathy with a desire to do something about it. "I feel so bad about my neighbor losing her family heirlooms in the flood. I understand how that feels as I lost some cherished family photos when my hard drive crashed. Let me ask her if there is something I can do to help."

The Reasonable Explanation

Let's review. Shannon asked Larry the following:

Shannon: "Can you help me understand what has caused you to arrive to work late?"

Larry: I'm sorry for coming in a few minutes late. I am trying my best to get here on time but I have some things that have come up that make that almost impossible right now. I am really frustrated.

Shannon: I'm sorry to hear that. Is there anything I can do for you?

Larry: Well, I never told you but my parents have been fighting a lot lately and have decided to get a divorce. This is not easy for me. I am an only child and I am still trying to pay off student debt so I live at home. Their constant fighting is taking a real toll on me.

Shannon: Wow, that sounds like a really difficult situation for you.

Larry: It is. I have had a really hard time with it and I turned to alcohol to help me cope with the constant arguments and the fear of how their separation will affect my life. I could go on but the point is that I got a DUI a few months ago because of it. I had been drinking to ignore the arguing one night but it got so bad that I just had to get out of the house. I got in my car to drive somewhere, I didn't even have a destination, it was just anywhere that wasn't home. As soon as I got to the corner, I must have run the stop sign and I got pulled over. It was obvious that I had been drinking so the police officer made me perform some field tests and he arrested me for DUI.

Shannon: That sounds frightening.

Larry: Yes. So I hired an attorney and paid money that I don't have; so much for paying off my student debt. I went to court and the judge ordered me to seek counseling or go to jail. It was hard but I finally found a counselor and the only time we could meet is early Tuesday and Thursday mornings. I am also not allowed to drive right now so I have to get a ride-share to pick me up and bring me to work. Sometimes, even though I do my best, this situation causes me to get to work a few minutes late. I come in feeling terrible and then when you point it out to me it makes me feel hopeless.

Shannon: I had no idea you were dealing with all of this. I am so sorry to hear about it. How can I help you?

Notice how Shannon responded to Larry's difficult situation with compassion? She expressed empathy, followed by an offer to help if she can. Larry truly is in a difficult situation and took a risk to open up to his boss and share some highly personal information. Shannon realized that this was a moment for her to be understanding. Not only is it the right thing to do, Larry will remember and appreciate her compassion for years to come.

If your personal management style is strict and no-nonsense, it does not excuse you from being compassionate. The most respected bosses are those who express genuine caring for their employees.

Improper Behavior

Sometimes, employees don't have a good explanation for their actions. Let's again revisit Shannon when she asked Larry the following:

Shannon: "Can you help me understand what has caused you to arrive to work late?"

Larry: I'm just late. I'm trying but you know how it is, you just arrive late sometimes.

Shannon: I realize that it can be hard to always show up everywhere on time. It is important that you arrive to work on time for the reasons I shared already.

Larry: I've never been the best at waking up early, especially when I like to go out with friends at night. I set an alarm but sometimes I just shut it off without even realizing it. By the time I get up, I rush as fast as I can but I get here late sometimes.

Larry was at least honest here. While his explanation does not absolve him from arriving to work on time, at least he gave Shannon something to work with. Now Shannon knows the reason that Larry is late and she can work with him to find a solution to the clearly identified problem. If Larry really wanted to try to get away with something he probably would have deflected when answering rather than providing a clear explanation.

Deflecting

A third, and often too common response to the question: "Can you help me understand what has caused you to arrive to work late?" is a deflection.

There are three common deflections; minimizing, otherizing and reverse blame. When an employee deflects blame, they are either trying to hide something very personal or possibly embarrassing to them or they really have no viable excuse for their actions. By answering with a deflection, they hope to change the subject of the conversation. If the manager takes the bait, the employee has been successful in laying the groundwork for an argument and the manager is playing defense. Using compassionate enquiry, the manager will never play defense.

Let's take a look at some examples.

Minimizing

Minimizing is when the employee minimizes the effects of their behaviors. For example:

Shannon: "Can you help me understand what has caused you to arrive to work late?"

Larry: It's only a few minutes late, what's the big deal. I am really here on time if you weren't so technical about it.

Shannon: It actually is a big deal. Whether it's one, five or ten minutes, you're still late.

Uh-oh, Shannon took the bait. Larry deflected with a minimization and Shannon found herself playing defense. The conversation may quickly devolve from this point into an argument over semantics.

Larry: Oh, come on, even if I was here exactly at 10:00 am, by the time I put my things in my locker and my lunch in the lunchroom, ten minutes have easily passed. You're making it sound like I barely showed up for work.

Shannon: Maybe so but that's not the point; you are supposed to be here on time.

Once Shannon took Larry's bait, she effectively lost control of the conversation. Now she is in a weak position and needs to try to find a way to dig herself out of it.

Otherizing

Otherizing is when the employee attempts to deflect the blame to others. The logic is that if the employee can deflect the conversation to focus on the bad behavior of others, then the employee should be absolved of all blame. For example:

Shannon: "Can you help me understand what has caused you to arrive to work late?"

Larry: Are you serious? Charlene comes in later than me lots of times.

Shannon: She does not. Charlene only came in late one time when she had a flat tire.

Larry: Oh yeah? Well what about Marcus? I watch him come in whenever he pleases. I guess it pays to be the boss's nephew.

Shannon: I don't control Marcus.

Larry: Well, then why are you trying to control me?

Again, Shannon took Larry's bait and lost control of the conversation. Larry was successful in turning an enquiry about his tardiness into a debate about the benefits of nepotism. Larry now has the moral high ground. Afterall, if Shannon doesn't hold Marcus accountable, why should she think that she can hold Larry accountable?

Reverse Blame

Reverse blame occurs when the employee turns from the attacked to the attacker. This technique can be very effective at putting the manager on the defensive. It is very easy to do and is often employed without conscious thought. Let's look at an example:

Shannon: "Can you help me understand what has caused you to arrive to work late?"

Larry: Why are you picking on me? You're always trying to find something to harass me about. You're late sometimes too, I've seen it.

Shannon: I am not picking on you and I am not late. You don't know what I have to do in the mornings. Just because you don't see me working doesn't mean that I'm not working.

Larry: Exactly my point. You assume that I'm not working and then you are quick to blame me. In my view, that's just picking on me and it's not right.

Shannon may even start to question herself and her motives at this point. Is she being unfair to Larry? Has she jumped to conclusions?

Wait a minute, she's not being unfair. Shannon was being very fair. In fact she just asked Larry to help her understand what caused him to arrive to work late on specific dates and times. She wasn't making any assumptions at all. She simply stated facts and properly enquired about an explanation. Larry artfully turned the tables on her. He dodged the question and put Shannon on the defensive, exactly where he wanted her.

Responding to Deflections - "The A - Loop"

Deflections are very powerful. We have seen examples of the most common deflections and how enticing they can be for the manager to take the bait. Deflections are probably the one thing that can most easily derail a compassionate enquiry. Once the manager takes the bait, they lose control over the enquiry and fall right into the losing end of an argument. But what can a manager do? It seems like Shannon's responses in the examples above were appropriate. What else is she to say? She has to defend herself and set Larry straight, doesn't she? She can't let him get away with it.

The problem is that by engaging in the conversation and taking a defensive role, Shannon will most likely not win. And what does "win" even mean here? Does she win if she comes up with a zinger and puts Larry in his place? How about if she screams louder or argues longer until Larry gives up? Is that winning?

The point is that in compassionate enquiry, the goal is not to win. The goal is to appropriately and effectively collect information to address and resolve a conduct or performance issue.

The good news is that there is a powerful and iron-clad method a manager can use to respond to any possible deflection and keep the conversation on track. This method is called the "A-Loop." In order to fully comprehend the "A-Loop" which will be discussed in the next chapter, it is necessary to first understand the next step in the compassionate enquiry process - Acknowledge.

CHAPTER 5:

Acknowledgement

To acknowledge is to make it known to the other party that you have received their message. It is easy to dismiss this step in the process as unnecessary. This step, like every step in the compassionate enquiry process, exists for a reason and if skipped, will cause the process to fail.

To acknowledge is easy; it simply requires the manager to state in response to the employee's explanation that "what I hear you saying is ..." followed by a paraphrase of what the employee has said. It let's the employee know that they have been heard and puts them in a place where they are ready to proceed with the enquiry conversation.

1. What I hear you saying is (paraphrase what the employee said.)

Let's look at an example of a conversation where acknowledgment is lacking.

Shannon: Larry, I heard you snap at that customer a while ago while you were on the register. We pride ourselves on customer service and you can't treat customers that way.

Larry: Did you hear what she said to me? She was frustrated that I was moving slowly because I was waiting for you to get me the price check and she called me a lazy, stupid employee. I am neither lazy nor stupid and I will not accept that type of language from anybody. If you had gotten off of your phone and got me the price check more quickly, that wouldn't have happened anyway.

Shannon: Oh, now it's my fault? For your information, that was the owner who called me while I was doing the price check and I had to answer. She kept me on the phone and I got you the price as quickly as I could.

Larry: (Raising his voice) So it's my fault that you answered your phone and didn't get me the price? You know how these customers can get. You left me to the wolves.

Shannon: (Raising her voice) I said the owner called, I had to take the call. I got you the price as soon as I could.

Larry: (Even louder) That customer called me lazy and stupid and it was because of you.

Shannon: (Louder still) I had to take the owner's call!

That didn't go so well. Now Larry and Shannon are both fuming mad at each other and have basically stopped communicating.

Did you notice that they each kept repeating the same basic message and incrementally raised their voices while doing so? Why is that? Why do arguments often turn into screaming matches? Do you really want to know? It's because each party feels as if the other party has not heard them so they feel that if they raise their voice, maybe they will get their message through. But it never seems to work. They raise their voices as loud as they can and get angrier and angrier until they throw their hands up in exasperation, cut off all communication and walk away.

This scenario results in hurt feelings on both sides followed by the parties finding it difficult to communicate any further. If the argument is not resolved, it can fester and permanently destroy a relationship. This happens far too many times in interpersonal relationships, be they marriages or workplace relationships between managers and employees or between two employees.

The good news is that this breakdown in communication will not happen if the parties simply learn to acknowledge each other. Let's take a look at the prior scenario and see how it would go if the parties acknowledged each other.

Shannon: Larry, I heard you snap at that customer a while ago while you were on the register. We pride ourselves on customer service and you can't treat customers that way.

Larry: Did you hear what she said to me? She was frustrated that I was moving slowly because I was waiting for you to get me the price check and she called me a lazy, stupid employee. I am neither lazy nor stupid and I will not accept that type of language from anybody. If you had gotten off of your phone and got me the price check more quickly, that wouldn't have happened anyway.

Shannon: What I hear you saying is that you snapped at the customer because she called you lazy and stupid and the reason you were taking extra time serving her was because you were waiting for me to get you a price check.

Larry: Yes, that's right.

Shannon: Well, we should talk about other ways that you can deal with a customer who calls you names.

Larry: I'm all ears but I don't like to be disrespected.

Well, that's a very different conversation now, isn't it? Once Shannon acknowledged Larry's concerns, the conversation easily turned to a problem solving discussion instead of a heated argument.

Emotions

Emotions are very personal for the speaker. When the speaker shares an emotion, they are sharing something deeply meaningful about their reaction to a situation. If you fail to properly acknowledge an emotion the other party will make sure that you realize your error. A failure here can convey the impression that you are not really listening at all.

The guidance above teaching you to acknowledge a statement by saying "what I hear you saying is …" followed by a paraphrase of what the employee has said is correct with the exception of when you are acknowledging an emotion. Emotions should never be paraphrased, they should be acknowledged exactly as spoken. If they are not, be prepared for the speaker to correct you.

Let's see how Shannon handles this.

Larry: That customer made me furious when she called me lazy and stupid.

Shannon: What I hear you saying is that the customer made you upset when she spoke with you and called you names.

Larry: No, she didn't make me "upset", I said she made me *furious*! Were you even listening to me?

Upset is not the same as furious and Larry did not agree with Shannon when she minimized his feelings. He used the word furious because he was *furious*! Shannon should have acknowledged Larry's emotion exactly how he stated it. When she failed, he was quick to set her straight.

Acknowledge reasonable explanation

Let's revisit Larry's original explanation about how the fallout from his DUI was making him late to work.

Shannon: "Can you help me understand what has caused you to arrive to work late?"

Larry: I'm sorry for coming in a few minutes late. I am trying my best to get here on time but I have some things that have come up that make that almost impossible right now. I am really frustrated.

Shannon: I'm sorry to hear that. Is there anything I can do for you?

Larry: Well, I never told you but my parents have been fighting a lot lately and have decided to get a divorce. This is not easy for me. I am an only child and I am still trying to pay off student debt so I live at home. Their constant fighting is taking a real toll on me.

Shannon: Wow, that sounds like a really difficult situation for you.

Larry: It is. I have had a really hard time with it and I turned to alcohol to help me cope with the constant arguments and the fear of how their separation will affect my life. I could go on but the point is that I got a DUI a few months ago because of it. I had been drinking to ignore the arguing one night but it got so bad that I just had to get out of the house. I got in my car to drive somewhere, I didn't even have a destination, it was just anywhere that wasn't home. As soon as I got to the corner, I must have run the stop sign and a cop pulled me over. It was obvious that I had been drinking so he made me perform some of those field tests and he arrested me for DUI.

Shannon did a great job of listening to Larry's explanation and expressing empathy and compassion. These steps are necessary because Larry is human after all. He has feelings and could use some support at a difficult time in his life.

Because Shannon was understanding and expressed a willingness to listen, Larry shared a great deal about his situation. He wasn't asking Shannon to fix it for him, nor was he asking her to be his therapist. Larry simply needed for her to listen so that she could understand his situation.

Now it is time for Shannon to acknowledge Larry's explanation. Larry shared a lot. Shannon's job is to acknowledge by paraphrasing the substance of his explanation, remembering to repeat his emotions exactly as stated.

Shannon: I hear that your parents have decided to divorce and their fighting makes you feel really frustrated. This led you to use alcohol to cope and now you have a DUI. As a result, you are seeing a counselor and that person is only available Tuesday and Thursday mornings which makes you late to work sometimes.

Great job! Shannon paraphrased the salient points of Larry's explanation and she remembered to repeat his emotion when he said that he was "frustrated." Now an actual conversation is taking place. There is no arguing or raised voices, just a dialogue about important facts. This is the path that can lead to a reasonable solution. The purpose of holding a compassionate enquiry is not to achieve victory but to make progress.

A-Loop

Acknowledgment seems pretty easy. Just listen to the other person and paraphrase back what you heard. But how can you acknowledge when the other person is deflecting? They're not providing any explanation so there is nothing to paraphrase.

When an employee uses a deflection, they are trying to get the manager to take the bait and shift the focus of the conversation to anything other than the issue at hand. The good news is that it is easy to avoid taking the bait and keep the enquiry on task by using the "A-Loop." The A-Loop simply allows the manager to acknowledge that the employee is deflecting and bring them back on task.

The A-Loop has two steps:

1) Acknowledge the deflection,

2) Remind the employee why you are speaking with them.

But out

One important note is to refrain from using the word "but" as a conjunction between the first and second steps of the A-Loop. When you use the word "but" it sounds as if you are simply dismissing everything that you just acknowledged. As we learned above, dismissive language works against you and reduces the ability to carry on a meaningful, productive conversation.

Minimizing

Using the A-Loop to respond to a deflection of minimizing would look like the following. Remember what Larry said before?

Shannon: "Can you help me understand what has caused you to arrive to work late?"

Larry: It's only a few minutes late, what's the big deal. I am really here on time if you weren't so technical about it.

Larry just deflected the conversation about his attendance by minimizing his actions.

Shannon will now use the A-Loop by acknowledging the deflection and reminding Larry why they are speaking.

Shannon: "I hear that you feel that a few minutes late is not a big deal." "We are here to speak about your attendance."

Notice the temptation you probably felt to insert the word "but" between the two statements? Read what Shannon said without using the word "but" and notice how the language is more concise and allows Shannon to be clear on what she is here to discuss.

Larry may not feel ready to discuss his attendance, especially if he has no good excuse for being late. He may try a different deflection.

Otherizing

Let's revisit how Larry used the deflection of otherizing.

Shannon: "Can you help me understand what has caused you to arrive to work late?"

Larry: Are you serious? Charlene comes in later than me lots of times.

Using the A-Loop, Shannon brings the conversation back to her stated objective; attendance.

Shannon: "I hear that you are concerned about Charlene's attendance." "We are here to speak about your attendance."

It looks like Larry is not having much success deflecting. Shannon is using the A-Loop and therefore does not feel the need to take Larry's bait. Perhaps he will try one more time.

Reverse Blame

Larry attempts to step up his game. He feels that he may be effective if he tries to put the blame back on Shannon.

Shannon: "Can you help me understand what has caused you to arrive to work late?"

Larry: Why are you picking on me? You're always trying to find something to harass me about. You're late sometimes too, I've seen it.

Again, Shannon refuses to take the bait and simply employs the A-Loop.

Shannon: "I hear that you feel that I am picking on you." "We are here to discuss your attendance."

By this point, Larry has a pretty good idea that deflections will not work with Shannon. He may try a few more times but as long as Shannon continues to use the A-Loop, she will keep the conversation on track.

Failure to Proceed

Some employees are so used to using deflections that they do not know what to do if their deflection fails. They simply either keep deflecting, hoping that the other party will blink first and eventually take the bait or one or both will get so frustrated that they will simply give up and walk away.

If an employee remains persistent in their attempts to deflect the conversation, there is no need to worry. The A-Loop will always work. Once the manager feels as though they have responded to enough deflections, they may simply move to the next step in the Compassionate Enquiry process. That step is to Resolve.

CHAPTER 6:

Coming to Resolution

To resolve is to find a solution to the problem that works for all parties.

When parties work together to craft their own solutions to a problem, they can develop unique and meaningful outcomes. A solution crafted by the parties allows for maximum creativity. If the parties choose not to participate in developing their own solution or if they are unsuccessful in doing so then a solution may be imposed upon them from an outside source.

"Us" is the solution

In the case we have been exploring where Larry was arriving to work late and did not have a reasonable explanation for his tardiness, the best person to craft a workable solution is Larry himself. This is because only Larry knows his unique circumstances and what solutions will be realistic given his personality and life responsibilities. The solution, to be workable, also has to meet management's needs. Therefore, it is always preferable to ask:

"What options are available to *us* to help you arrive to work on time?"

Notice the word "*us*" in the question. That word is intentional; it is an acknowledgement that both parties, employee and management, need to be part of the solution. If Shannon were to simply provide her own solution, it disempowers Larry and may not work with his reality. Let's see an example.

Shannon: Larry, since you have been arriving late, you need to get up earlier to get to work on time.

Larry: I already wake at 6:00 am.

Shannon's solution sounded completely reasonable. Get up earlier and you will have more time to get to work on time. Unfortunately, this solution is simplistic and may be ignoring Larry's reality. Shannon did not address the details. She does not know what time Larry wakes up currently. She does not know what Larry does between waking and leaving the house and she does not know what happens once Larry begins his commute. In short, Shannon has failed to diagnose the problem, she does not know what is causing Larry to be late, so she cannot be successful in crafting a meaningful solution.

The first step in crafting a solution is to understand the problem. In order to understand the problem, all Shannon has to do is ask.

Shannon: "What options are available to *us* to help you get to work on time?"

Larry: "I don't know, I'm trying but it's hard."

Shannon: "Would you mind sharing what you do between waking and arriving to work?

Larry: "Well, if you must know, I wake at 6:00 am and I get dressed to meet my marathon training partners. I am training for the New York marathon and we have been progressively running longer distances on Tuesdays and Thursdays. By time I get home, shower, get dressed for work and commute in, I am a few minutes late. Obviously I can't run any faster so that's what makes me late."

Shannon: "Thank you for sharing that with me. So the reason you are late is not because you are waking up late but because your marathon training schedule is conflicting with your work schedule."

Larry: "Yeah, I guess."

Shannon now knows the reason that Larry is arriving late to work. Armed with the specific problem that needs resolution, the conversation can now be more productive.

Shannon: "So, what options are available to *us* to help you get to work on time?"

Larry: "Well, I see this schedule is no longer workable for me. I've actually been considering what I can do about it but I like the group I run with and I guess I was just hoping I could make it work. Do you think you could change my shift so that I could start work an hour later?"

Shannon: "Yes, it sounds like your schedule is just not working for you anymore. Unfortunately, I can't change your shift so we have to find a different option."

Larry: "Well, to be honest, one of the other members of my training group has been having a similar problem getting to work late. His boss is on him about his tardiness too. We've talked about breaking off from the bigger group and either starting our training a little earlier or maybe doing it in the early evening after we get home from work."

Larry has just crafted his own solution that works for him. If he takes either of the proposed actions, he will have resolved the issue that was making him late to work. Shannon has no problem with either of the proposed solutions because she is getting what she needs; Larry will arrive to work on time.

Shannon's initial attempt to resolve the problem by telling Larry to simply wake up earlier would not have resulted in Larry getting to work any earlier. By working with Larry to craft his own solution, the problem was resolved in a way that Larry can accept and will buy into.

Employee Wellbeing

Shannon was successful in working with Larry to find a solution when his problem was caused by his marathon training schedule. What kind of solution is possible if Larry's problem was related to his parent's divorce, his DUI and related counseling?

Larry was arriving late to work because he was attending mandatory counseling sessions as a result of his receiving a DUI. He got charged with DUI due to the drinking he used to cope with some very difficult issues at home. One could say that it is not the employer's problem. We all have our own issues and it is our own personal responsibility to figure it out. The problem here is that those issues are affecting Larry's job. If he can find a good solution, he will be better equipped to focus on his job and his performance may not suffer. If the issues remain unresolved, Larry's mind will inevitably be on issues other than his job and both he and his employer will suffer the effects.

Larry shared a lot of information with Shannon because he was legitimately reaching out for her help. Some of the pertinent points Larry shared are:

- Larry is late on Tuesdays and Thursdays because he is seeing a court ordered counselor those mornings.

- Larry can't drive so he has to call a rideshare and sometimes that makes him late.

- Larry is seeing his counselor Tuesday and Thursday mornings because those were the only times available when he called.

- Larry is working with a lawyer to address the DUI charges.

Shannon: What options are available to *us* to help you get to work on time?

Larry: Well, thank you for asking. I want to get here on time and I have been working hard to figure it out. As I told you, I see my counselor Tuesday and Thursday mornings because that's the only opening she had. I have already asked her to put me on the waiting list for any appointments she has open up after I finish work. She expects that something may open up within the next two weeks. I am also working with my lawyer to try to get the case thrown out. He told me that since I have a clean record, and given the circumstances, he thinks he can convince the prosecutor to let me enter a pre-trial diversion program. I would agree to two months more of counseling and then if I stay clean, they will dismiss the case. So if you can work with me for just the next few weeks until my counseling appointments are moved, I should be able to put all of this behind me.

Shannon: Wow, that sounds like a lot on your shoulders. My problem is that I need somebody to be here no later than 10:00 am on Tuesdays and Thursdays.

Larry: I realize that and I am so sorry that I have to be late sometimes. If it helps, I explained my situation to Charlene and I asked if she wouldn't mind taking an earlier shift to cover for me on Tuesday and Thursday. This would just be for the next month and I will agree to work her schedule that starts later. Then, once my counseling appointments are changed to afternoons, we would go back to our regular schedules. She said that she would be willing to do that for me.

Shannon: Well, I appreciate you and Charlene working together and being proactive. That's what teamwork is all about.

Larry was responsible and did not want to be late to work, he just found himself in a difficult spot. By Shannon and Larry working together, Larry was able to offer a solution that worked for him and for Shannon. Larry will always remember how Shannon worked with him in his time of need. Their work relationship will most likely improve after this situation.

Uncooperative employees

It is always best when an employee participates in crafting the solution to their own problem. In most cases, they will. Unfortunately, some employees are unhappy that their manager is holding them accountable. They may be thinking that "they don't pay me enough to be here on time" or "As soon as I find another job, I'm leaving anyways." An employee with this mindset is less motivated to participate in finding a solution.

When an employee chooses not to participate in finding a solution to their problem, then the manager has no options left except to craft their own solution. This is exactly the case when an employee continues to deflect even after the manager uses the A-Loop several times. Fortunately, most employers have a progressive discipline policy designed to address these issues. Shannon gave Larry every opportunity to explain his situation and resolve it; he chose not to.

Shannon: "Larry, I have been willing to work with you to find a solution to your attendance issue but you have chosen not to cooperate. The only option left to me is to implement the company's progressive discipline process. I will therefore issue you a written warning this afternoon. I hope you will find a way to correct the situation. If not, I will be required to continue with the progressive discipline process. If you change your mind and would like for me to help you find a solution, please let me know."

Larry will now choose to find his own solution to the problem if he wants to avoid further discipline and perhaps eventually losing his job. If he chooses not to resolve the problem then there is not much more that Shannon can do.

Solving the unsolvable problem

Sometimes managers and employees would actually like to resolve a problem but simply find themselves stuck at an impasse. This can be very frustrating to both parties because each genuinely wants to identify a solution but they just can't see a path forward. Oftentimes when the solution seems non-existent it is because the parties are focused on their "positions." A position is best understood by thinking of it as *what* each party wants. Let's look at an example where Matt, a manager, needs Cheryl to stay late to complete a report.

A position is *what* a party wants.

Matt: "Cheryl, I hate to do this but you have to stay late today until you complete the financial report."

Cheryl: "I can't stay late today."

Uh-oh, we have a problem. Matt needs Cheryl to stay late but Cheryl says she can't stay late. Matt is the manager and he is responsible for ensuring that the financial report is complete on time. He has no choice but to clarify for Cheryl that she is the only one who can complete the report and must step up to do so.

This situation is headed for disaster. Matt feels trapped, he has to convince Cheryl to do her job. He feels that he asked nicely but was rebuffed. Matt is a manager so it is his job to address employee problems.

Matt: "You have to stay late to get the report done. You are a salaried employee and it is one of your job responsibilities."

Cheryl: "I'm sorry, if you had told me a few days ago, I would have tried to get it done for you but you are springing this on me at the last minute and I just can't stay tonight."

Matt: "Look Cheryl, I don't want to do this but as your manager, you have to stay or I will have to write you up. You know that the boss doesn't like people who are not team players."

Matt is taking an authoritarian approach. He is imposing a solution on Cheryl and she is not happy about it. The hard feelings generated in situations like this often fester for years and can permanently damage Matt and Cheryl's relationship. But Matt does not see any way out.

Matt and Cheryl are stuck because they are focused on their respective positions. Matt needs Cheryl to stay late and Cheryl can't stay late. It seems as if there is nowhere to go from here.

Become interested in a solution

Matt and Cheryl are stuck. Neither one wants an argument but the circumstances are putting them at odds with each other. There has to be a way out of this conundrum. The good news is that there probably is. Remember, Matt and Cheryl are stuck because their positions on staying late are at odds with each other and seem irreconcilable. Positions are statements of *what* each party wants.

The easiest way to break out of a deadlock in positional thinking is to look behind the position and explore each party's interests. Interests are *why* a party has their position. We know that Matt needs Cheryl to stay late. We also know that Cheryl can't stay late. What we don't know is why each party has their position.

Interests are *why* each party has their position.

Matt needs Cheryl to stay late because he has to turn in the financial report by 9:00 am tomorrow morning. Cheryl can't stay late because she is taking her daughter to a very important swimming competition where her daughter is favored to win a gold medal. Cheryl has nobody else to take her daughter to the competition and even if she did, she promised her daughter she would be there to root her on. Cheryl simply cannot ,and will not miss this competition.

It appears that Matt and Cheryl each have good reasons for their positions. How do you decide whose reason is more important? If the parties focused only on positions, this would be a very hard call. But when they focus on interests, solutions often appear.

Matt and Cheryl have each shared why they have their stated positions. Do you see any possible solutions here? Matt needs the report completed by 9:00 am tomorrow. Cheryl has to be at her daughter's competition right after work. Isn't it a reasonable possibility for Matt to ask Cheryl to work on the report after her daughter's competition or early in the morning? If she stays up to work on it tonight, he can let her sleep in late tomorrow.

Once the parties focused on their interests, a simple solution appeared.

Positions are what the parties want.

Interests are why they want it.

Suicide

No discussion about employee issues would be complete without a basic explanation on how managers should respond to an employee alluding to suicidal thoughts or threatening suicide. This is an issue none of us wants to think about yet we cannot ignore it. The fact is that some employees can feel so desperate about their circumstances that they see suicide as their only way out.

Managers are not mental health counselors and reading a few paragraphs in this book about suicide will not train you to be such. However, it is imperative that managers know how to recognize suicidal thinking and have a plan on how to address it.

It is not uncommon for employees to use figures of speech sometimes like "I can't believe I did so poorly on that presentation, I'm so embarrassed I could kill myself." These statements are not serious threats of suicide. However, there are other times when employees exhibit warning signs and language that should be of legitimate concern.

Warning Signs for Suicide[1]

- Talking about wanting to die or to kill themselves

- Looking for a way to kill themselves, like searching online or buying a gun

- Talking about feeling hopeless or having no reason to live

- Talking about feeling trapped or in unbearable pain

- Talking about being a burden to others

- Increasing the use of alcohol or drugs

- Acting anxious or agitated; behaving recklessly

- Sleeping too little or too much

- Withdrawing or isolating themselves

- Showing rage or talking about seeking revenge

- Extreme mood swings

Risk Factors for Suicide

- Mental disorders, particularly mood disorders, schizophrenia, anxiety disorders, and certain personality disorders

---

[1] www.suicidelifeline.org

- Alcohol and other substance use disorders

- Hopelessness

- Impulsive and/or aggressive tendencies

- History of trauma or abuse

- Major physical illnesses

- Previous suicide attempt(s)

- Family history of suicide

- Job or financial loss

- Loss of relationship(s)

- Easy access to lethal means

- Local clusters of suicide

- Lack of social support and sense of isolation

- Stigma associated with asking for help

- Lack of healthcare, especially mental health and substance abuse treatment

- Cultural and religious beliefs, such as the belief that suicide is a noble resolution of a personal dilemma

- Exposure to others who have died by suicide (in real life or via the media and Internet)

If an employee has any risk factors or exhibits any of the warning signs above, it is important to address them.

Statements like "None of this matters because I won't be around after tomorrow." or "I don't care, I don't have any reason to live anyway" should not be ignored.

If an employee seems to be threatening suicide, it is important to ask them about it directly. Suicide is an uncomfortable issue and some people fear that if they say the word *suicide*, it may somehow put the thought into the other person's head. Nobody wants to feel responsible for "causing" someone to commit suicide. The reality is that a failure to appropriately address the issue results in the loss of an opportunity to encourage the suicidal employee to seek help.

It is important to ask directly a version of "Are you thinking of committing suicide?" The temptation exists to try to minimize the situation mostly to make the speaker feel more comfortable. A common question aksed that is not helpful is: "You wouldn't do anything stupid, would you." To a suicidal person, their thoughts are rational, not stupid. The only way out of their situation that they can find is to commit suicide; so no, they wouldn't do anything stupid but they may do something they see as rational.

After inquiring "Are you thinking of killing yourself?" if their answer is not a clear "no" then stay with that person and help them find assistance. Some employers have a Human Resources staff trained to assist in these situations. There may be a company Employee Assistance Program, a family member to call or even a suicide prevention hotline or a call to 911. The point is to stay with the employee until they receive appropriate assistance.

The good news is that if you practice Compassionate Enquiry, the process will automatically help you with this situation. Let's see how:

I - Initiate. State the issue followed by specific supporting facts.

William: Cindy, I would like to speak with you about your performance.

Cindy: Sure.

William: I've noticed that over the last few days you've seemed preoccupied with something. On Monday it looked like you were staring off into space during the staff meeting. On Tuesday I crossed paths with you several times and you seemed to have a blank look on your face. And today, when you came into my office, it looked like you had been crying.

C - Clarify. Clarify why the conversation is important to you and seek clarification from the other party about their actions.

William: When I see these signs, it makes me concerned that you are not feeling your best and may need someone to talk to. Can you help me understand what might be going on for you?

Cindy: (crying) It just feels like the world is crashing in on me. I know the company is going through a merger and I am afraid I will lose my job. At my age I don't think I can find another job and as a single parent I have three kids to raise. Money has always been tight and I don't want my kids to see me fail them. I feel so useless that my kids are better off if I were dead. At least I was smart enough to purchase a life insurance policy.

William: I am so sorry to hear that you are dealing with all of that. Are you thinking of killing yourself?

Cindy: Well, do you see any better way? (breaks down crying harder) At least in death I can provide my kids what I couldn't provide by living.

At this point of the Enquiry, William knows that he should not leave Cindy alone. His sole responsibility is to assist Cindy in finding help. William knows that his company has an Employee Assistance program.

William: Cindy, I care very much about you. We have an Employee Assistance Program staffed with professionals who can speak with you and help you process all of this. Would you like to use my office and call them or would you like me to call them for you?

But wait, it seems like William is not giving Cindy a choice over her own life. While it is generally best to always allow, and even encourage employees to participate in decisions that affect them, in this case, Cindy is not thinking clearly.

She is suicidal. She cannot be relied upon to process everything rationally. The consequences of William failing to take action could be that Cindy kills herself. There is no return from such action. Cindy may be upset with William but she will be alive. In reality she will most likely thank him once she has a chance to speak with a counselor and work through her issues.

CHAPTER 7:

Seeing Eye to Eye

"E" stands for "Eye to eye"

Once the parties reach a resolution, it is important to make sure that they each have the same understanding. This is accomplished by asking the employee to "please explain our understanding to me in your own words."

Please explain our understanding to me in your own words.

If the parties are not seeing eye to eye, they may each leave with different expectations. This one simple question ensures that both parties are leaving with the same expectations. A misunderstanding due to unconfirmed expectations can lead to one or both parties feeling that the other has failed to comply with the agreement.

Let's examine the agreement between Matt and Cheryl about the report. It appears that Cheryl will agree to work on the report either after her daughter's competition or early the next morning. If she can get it done, Matt may agree to let Cheryl sleep in late the next day. An examination of each of their understandings leads to the following situation.

Matt believes that Cheryl is going to complete the report after her daughter's competition this evening. That works great for him because he plans to wake up early at 5:00 am to find the report in his inbox so that he can review it before he turns it in. In exchange, he is perfectly fine allowing Cheryl to sleep in an extra two hours until 9:00 am the next day.

Cheryl is now relieved because she feels that she can go to her daughter's competition and then take her daughter out for a surprise celebratory dessert once she is done. She may be home late but that's OK because she will wake up in the morning at her regular time, 7:00 am, complete the report and then go back to bed until noon to catch up on needed sleep.

The problem here should be obvious. Because Matt and Cheryl did not check to ensure they both saw Eye to Eye on their solution, Matt is going to expect to find the report in his inbox at 5:00 am where Cheryl doesn't expect to even begin working on it until the next day at 7:00 am.

It is easy to understand how Matt will be upset when he finds his inbox empty at 5:00 am and call Cheryl, waking her the next day complaining that he does not have the report. Cheryl will be taken by surprise because she was under the impression that she could work on the report at 7:00 am and then get some needed rest. Cheryl will then have to get up at 5:00 am, scramble to complete the report for Matt earlier than she had planned and probably end up forfeiting the extra sleep she had planned to get that morning.

Had Matt simply asked Cheryl to "please explain our understanding to me in your own words" before concluding the conversation, this simple but common error would have been exposed so they could clarify it and prevent any misunderstanding.

CHAPTER 8:

Practice Exercises

Now that you have an understanding of the Compassionate Enquiry process, it is time to practice. I have found that actually working through exercises helps to significantly increase the reader's confidence and competence with the material. Please follow the exercises below and resist the attempt to read ahead until you have formulated your own answer. This is the best way to ensure for yourself that you are mastering the material.

Initiate

Remember in the initiate phase that you want to accomplish two important tasks; 1) inform the other party what you would like to speak with them about and 2) follow that up with supporting facts. In many cases it can be difficult to differentiate fact from opinion. If you deviate from stating pure fact, you open the door to argument over interpretation of words that are based upon an individual opinion.

The steps of this process are as follows:

1) "I would like to speak with you about (topic)."
2) (Recite supporting facts.)

Review the following examples and then try to recite a proper initiation statement based solely upon fact.

Delivering confusion

Donald works for a national delivery company. In his job, he arrives to work and is assigned a delivery van that has been loaded for him overnight. His job is to drive his assigned route and deliver all of the packages in his van by the end of his shift. His employer has studied approximately how long it should take for him to deliver each package and they keep metrics to make sure that their employees are optimizing their time.

Donald recently was assigned to a new manager who has noticed some issues that he feels require attention. Over the last month, the company has received several calls from customers complaining that they either had not received their order or that they had received something that they had not ordered. Specifically, a customer who lives on 32nd avenue called in to say that they had not received their package but their neighbor on 32nd court had hand-delivered their package to them because it had been delivered to the neighbor's address. There were also two more complaints that came from the Timberwood apartment complex from customers in the 400 building whose packages apparently were delivered to the 500 building. Finally, there were three other complaints from customers who stated that they had not received their packages even though the driver reported in the online system stated that those packages had been delivered.

What would an appropriate initiation statement look like?

Please write your answer on a separate piece of paper before referring to the proposed answer below.

Proposed answer

Donald, I would like to speak with you about the accuracy of your deliveries.

Since I have taken over as manager I have received a complaint from the individual who lives on 32nd Ave. who reported that their neighbor who lives on 32nd Court had received their package. I also have received two complaints from the Timberwood apartment complex from customers in the 400 building who reported that their packages were delivered to the 500 building. Finally, I have received three additional complaints from customers who stated that they had not received their packages at all but when they check the delivery app it shows that their packages were reported as delivered.

You're showing too much

Sandra works at her local community college as a graduate assistant. She is doing this job to help pay for her education. She performs numerous different tasks throughout the semester and at the end of each semester it is her job to print out grade reports for each student and post them on the physical grade board. The college does not have a large budget and is working with antiquated systems that are in need of upgrades. However, they have to work with what they have and Sandra has been instructed that when she pulls up individual student's grade records, she is to manually remove each student's name and Social Security number and replace that information with the appropriate student ID. This way, when grades are posted to the board, each student's privacy is protected.

At the end of last semester, Sandra's boss received multiple complaints about student's private information being posted on the public grade board. One student, Patricia Jennings, found that both her name and Social Security number were posted publicly. A few weeks later she found that somebody had applied for credit cards in her name and she believes that person found her Social Security number and name posted by the school. A second student, Grayson Chamblee found that his full name was posted along with his failing grade in chemistry. He was devastated when he found that his friends saw the information and they further shared it on social media. Finally, Claudia Jimenez complained about her name and Social Security number being posted to the board.

What would an appropriate initiation statement look like?

Please write your answer on a separate piece of paper before referring to the proposed answer below.

Proposed answer

Sandra, I would like to speak with you about some accuracy issues related to posting of grades.

I trained you to make sure that when you post a student's grades that you remove their name and Social Security number and replace it with their student number before you put it on the public grade board. This last semester I received a complaint from Patricia Jennings who found her name and Social Security number both posted publicly. Apparently shortly thereafter she found that somebody had applied for a credit card in her name. Secondly, Grayson

Chamblee also found that his full name, but no Social Security number, was posted along with his failing grade in chemistry. Someone took a photo of that grade and shared it on social media. Finally, Claudia Jimenez complained to me that she found that her full name and Social Security number were posted publicly.

You're too slow

Peter works in the IT department of a midsize company with offices that occupy five floors of a downtown high-rise office building. His job is to resolve employee's technical support requests. There are members of the IT department who are assigned to work on software issues which can sometimes be complicated and take significant effort to resolve. Peter, however, specifically addresses only hardware issues which are typically easier to resolve and involve replacing a broken mouse, providing appropriate cables to connect printers and other hardware devices to computers and retrieve and replace broken monitors or keyboards.

Peter has a new manager who recently joined the company and is not familiar with the systems or processes yet. The manager has been monitoring how much time it takes employees to complete their tasks and he has some concerns about how long it takes Peter to complete seemingly simple tasks. A few issues that concern the manager are that last Tuesday Peter was to deliver a replacement mouse to an employee one floor below him. It took Peter over an hour to complete this task. The second issue occurred last Wednesday when Peter was supposed to bring an upgraded monitor to an employee on the fifth floor. It took him two hours to complete this task. Finally, this morning Peter needed to replace a broken power cord for an employee on his same floor and it took him 45 minutes to complete that task.

What would an appropriate initiation statement look like?

Please write your answer on a separate piece of paper before referring to the proposed answer below.

Proposed answer

Peter, I'd like to speak with you about how long it takes you to complete your tasks.

I noticed that last Tuesday you were assigned to deliver a replacement mouse to an employee one floor below you and it took you over an hour. Similarly, last Wednesday you were supposed to provide an upgraded monitor to an employee on the fifth floor and that took you almost 2 hours to complete. Finally, this morning you had to replace a broken power cord for an employee on the same floor where you work and it took you almost 45 minutes.

Do you care?

Albert recently graduated with his nursing degree and got his first job at the local hospital. He was always extra careful to make sure that he followed a doctor's orders because he did not want to make any mistakes and harm a patient. Late last Friday night a new patient, Laura was admitted to the hospital and Albert was assigned to care for her. The doctor had met with the patient earlier during the admission process and wrote medication orders in the patient's chart. Albert was careful to read the orders and saw that the doctor had ordered penicillin for the patient to be given twice a day, once at 7:00 AM and again at 7:00 PM.

Albert made sure that he gathered the correct medication at the correct dose and administered it to the patient specifically as ordered. After the first dose, the patient complained to Albert that she was not feeling right. She had a rash and her back was itching. Albert made sure to address the patient's concern and applied an ointment to help reduce the itching. That evening, Albert gave the second dose of penicillin to the patient as ordered. A few hours later the patient again began to complain of severe itching and a rash. Again, Albert applied the ointment to help reduce the itching.

When Albert completed his shift, he briefed the incoming nurse on the patient's situation. The incoming nurse,

Damita, questioned Albert about the patient's rash and itching and realized that the patient was having an allergic reaction to the penicillin. Damita notified her manager about the patient's apparent allergic reaction and expressed her concern that Albert had missed this important sign. The manager realized that she needed to speak with Albert about the situation.

What would an appropriate initiation statement look like?

Please write your answer on a separate piece of paper before referring to the proposed answer below.

Proposed answer

Albert, I would like to speak with you about appropriate patient care.

Last Friday night you were assigned to care for a new patient, Laura. Her doctor prescribed penicillin to be given twice a day. You administered the penicillin as ordered and after each administration your patient complained of itching and a rash. You addressed the situation by applying an ointment to reduce the itching.

Clarify

After we initiate the conversation, the next step is to clarify why the conversation is important to you. Then you will seek clarification from the other party about their actions.

Remember, there are two distinct steps required when you clarify. First, you will explain why the issue is important enough for you to be addressing it. Next you will seek to gain a better understanding of the other person's actions by specifically asking for their explanation as to why they took their actions.

The steps of this process are as follows:

1) "When you (do the thing we are discussing) it causes (the negative outcome I wish to avoid)"

2) "Can you help me understand what is causing you to (do the things we are discussing)?

Now re-read the scenarios for "Delivering confusion," "You're showing too much," "You're too slow," and "Do you care." Then write your answer for each on a separate piece of paper before reading the proposed response. You will have to create your own explanation when developing your response to the first part but it should logically follow from the facts. What matters is that you follow the appropriate format and stay factual. Avoid being accusatory because that can cause the other person to unnecessarily become defensive.

Delivering confusion

Proposed answer

When you deliver packages to the wrong address it makes our customers upset with us, they do not receive their items, which can sometimes be important, such as medications, and it costs us time and money since we have to address customer service calls and track down and re-deliver packages.

Can you help me understand what is causing you to deliver packages to the wrong addresses?

You're showing too much

Proposed answer

When you post a student's identifying information, it causes a violation of their privacy and our own privacy policy, can cause them embarrassment, may lead to identity theft and could get us sued.

Can you help me understand what is causing you to sometimes post a student's name or social security number?

You're too slow

Proposed answer

When it takes a long time to complete a task, it causes other tasks to get backed up. That means that some of our employees literally have to stop work while they wait for you to deliver IT support. That causes a cascading effect because other employees are waiting for their output which can literally slow down multiple steps in a project.

Can you help me understand what is causing you to take the amount of time you take to complete your tasks?

Notice here that we did not ask Peter to explain "... what is causing you to take *excessive* time to complete your tasks?" Excessive is an accusation that can make the other defensive. Peter has not had a chance to give his explanation yet. He may or may not have a perfectly reasonable answer to explain why each task takes the amount f time that it does. After he provides a response, then you can make the decision whether he is taking *excessive* amounts of time to complete a task.

Do you care?

Proposed answer

When you fail to recognize the signs of a patient's allergic reaction to a medication it can be life threatening to that patient and create a liability for the hospital.

Can you help me understand what caused you to fail to report signs of an allergic reaction and administer a second dose of Penicillin to patient Laura?

A-Loop

The A-Loop is used to address an employee who is using deflecting responses. It is a very powerful tool that allows the manager to remain in control of the conversation. The A-Loop is relatively simple to use but since it is a new way of responding, I find that most students need to practice it out loud until they become comfortable with it. It can be hard to resist the urge to "take the bait" of the deflection and thus respond to a statement that we find to be absurd or hurtful. That's the point! The more absurd or hurtful the statement is, the more likely the manager is to take the bait and thus take the heat off the employee.

The A-Loop has two steps:

1) Acknowledge the deflection,
2) Remind the employee why you are speaking with them.

Take some time to practice the A-Loop. Find a partner to help you with this exercise. Read the four scenarios above one at a time first by stating the initiation statement followed by the clarify statement. Then ask your partner to respond to the clarify statement by using each of the common deflections of minimizing, otherizing and reverse blame. Respond to each deflection with the A-Loop and remember to "but-out" by refraining from using the word "but" as a transition.

Delivering Confusion

In the "Delivering confusion" scenario you would say:

Initiation

Donald, I would like to speak with you about the accuracy of your deliveries.

Since I have taken over as manager I have received a complaint from the individual who lives on 32nd Ave. who reported that their neighbor who lives on 32nd Court had received their package. I also have received two complaints from the Timberwood apartment complex from customers in the 400 building who reported that their packages were delivered to the 500 building. Finally, I have received three additional complaints from customers who stated that they had not received their packages at all but when they check the delivery app it shows that their packages were reported as delivered.

Clarification

When you deliver packages to the wrong address it makes our customers upset with us, they do not receive their items, which can sometimes be important, such as medications, and it costs us time and money since we have to address customer service calls and track down and re-deliver packages.

Can you help me understand what is causing you to deliver packages to the wrong addresses?

A-Loop

Then your partner would respond with each type of deflection:

Minimizing: "It's only a few packages, what's the big deal?"

A-Loop: "I understand that you feel it is only a few packages." "We are here to talk about improving the accuracy of your deliveries."

Otherizing: "Raul misbelievers packages too but I don't see you talking to him."

A-Loop: "I understand that you feel Raul misbelievers packages too." We are here to talk about improving the accuracy of your deliveries."

Reverse blame: "Why are you always picking on me? You're not perfect either, you know."

A-Loop: "I understand that you feel that I am not perfect and make mistakes." "We are here to talk about improving the accuracy of your deliveries."

You're showing too much

In the "You're showing too much" scenario you would say:

Initiation

Sandra, I would like to speak with you about some accuracy issues related to posting of grades.

I trained you to make sure that when you post a student's grades that you remove their name and Social Security number and replace it with their student number before you put it on the public grade board. This last semester I received a complaint from Patricia Jennings who found her name and Social Security number both posted publicly. Apparently shortly thereafter she found that somebody had applied for a credit card in her name. Secondly, Grayson Chamblee also found that his full name, but no Social Security number, was posted along with his failing grade in chemistry. Someone took a photo of that grade and shared it on social media. Finally, Claudia Jimenez complained to me that she found that her full name and Social Security number were posted publicly.

Clarification

When you post a student's identifying information, it causes a violation of their privacy and our own privacy policy, can cause them embarrassment, may lead to identity theft and could get us sued.

Can you help me understand what is causing you to sometimes post a student's name or social security number?

A-Loop

Then your partner would respond with each type of deflection:

Minimizing: "It's only a few minor errors, what's the big deal?"

A-Loop: "I understand that you feel it is only a few minor errors." "We are here to talk about improving the accuracy of your postings."

Otherizing: "Every other employee here makes mistakes too but I don't see you talking to them."

A-Loop: "I understand that you feel that every other employee here makes mistakes too." We are here to talk about improving the accuracy of your postings."

Reverse blame: "Why are you obsessed with me and my work?"

A-Loop: "I understand that you feel that I am obsessed with you and your work." "We are here to talk about improving the accuracy of your postings."

You're too slow

In the "You're too slow" scenario you would say:

INITIATION

Peter, I'd like to speak with you about how long it takes you to complete your tasks.

I noticed that last Tuesday you were assigned to deliver a replacement mouse to an employee one floor below you and it took you over an hour. Similarly, last Wednesday you were supposed to provide an upgraded monitor to an employee on the fifth floor and that took you almost 2 hours to complete. Finally, this morning you had to replace a broken power cord for an employee on the same floor where you work and it took you almost 45 minutes.

Clarification

When it takes a long time to complete a task, it causes other tasks to get backed up. That means that some of our employees literally have to stop work while they wait for you to deliver IT support. That causes a cascading effect because other employees are waiting for their output which can literally slow down multiple steps in a project.

Can you help me understand what is causing you to take the amount of time you take to complete your tasks?

A-Loop

Then your partner would respond with each type of deflection:

Minimizing: "I'm really not taking long at all when you look at the big picture."

A-Loop: "I understand that you feel you are not really taking long at all." "We are here to talk about completing your tasks in a timely manner."

Otherizing: "Everybody else takes as long or longer than me to complete their tasks."

A-Loop: "I understand that you feel that everybody else takes as long or longer than you to complete their tasks." We are here to talk about completing your tasks in a timely manner."

Reverse blame: "I bet you couldn't do it any faster than me."

A-Loop: "I understand that you feel that I could not complete your tasks any faster than you." "We are here to talk about completing your tasks in a timely manner."

Do you care

In the "Do you care" scenario you would say:

Initiation

Albert, I would like to speak with you about appropriate patient care.

Last Friday night you were assigned to care for a new patient, Laura. Her doctor prescribed penicillin to be given twice a day. You administered the penicillin as ordered and after each administration your patient complained of itching and a rash. You addressed the situation by applying an ointment to reduce the itching.

Clarification

When you fail to recognize the signs of a patient's allergic reaction to a medication it can be life threatening to that patient and create a liability for the hospital.

Can you help me understand what caused you to fail to report signs of an allergic reaction and administer a second dose of Penicillin to patient Laura?

A-Loop

Then your partner would respond with each type of deflection:

Minimizing: "The patient is fine, nothing happened to her."

A-Loop: "I understand that you feel that the patient is fine and nothing happened to her." "We are here to talk about you delivering appropriate patient care."

Otherizing: "Marissa gave the wrong medicine to her patient and almost killed her. What aren't you talking to her?"

A-Loop: "I understand that you are concerned about Marissa's patient care." We are here to talk about you delivering appropriate patient care."

Reverse blame: "You act as if you're perfect."

A-Loop: "I understand that you feel that I am acting as if I'm perfect." "We are here to talk about you delivering appropriate patient care."

Now that you've completed the exercise, you probably found that it's harder to do than it seems. However, the more you practice it, the easier it becomes. Eventually, if you continue to practice, the A-Loop skills can become automatic.

About the Author:

Andrew E. Colsky, JD, LLM, LPC is an attorney, coach, mediator and mental health counselor. He has continuously managed workplace disputes since the early 1990's and has experience designing conflict management systems for some of the largest organizations in the country. In addition to private sector clients, he has worked with the United States Postal Service as an attorney focused on alternative dispute resolution and as part of the task force that implemented their REDRESS program. He has also worked on contract with the US Department of State, the United States Department of Justice, and in-house with the Transportation Security Administration to address workplace conflicts.

Mr. Colsky served as a former Chair of the United States ADR Steering Committee reporting to the US Attorney General and Chair of the Workplace ADR section for all Cabinet level agencies. Over his career he has mediated hundreds of workplace disputes. He has also trained mediators in both the public and private sectors.

Mr. Colsky merged his knowledge of law and mental health to develop Compassionate Enquiry. To accomplish this, he drew from decades of experience with workplace disputes and identified the most common issues that led to both positive and negative outcomes. He realized that there was indeed a better way to address these matters from their very genesis.

It is important for us all to realize that we never know what is going on for a person in their personal life. In too many cases, employees' home lives impact their work performance yet employers turn a blind eye. Yes, employees are responsible for getting their work done correctly and timely but they are also human beings. By using the Compassionate Enquiry process, employers are properly equipped to manage any situation.